Other books by Peter Jay

Poetry

LIFELINES

SHIFTING FRONTIERS

Editions

THE GREEK ANTHOLOGY

SAPPHO THROUGH ENGLISH POETRY
with Caroline Lewis

Translations

Ana Blandiana
THE HOUR OF SAND
with Anca Cristofovici

Ştefan Aug. Doinaş
ALIBI AND OTHER POEMS
with Virgil Nemoianu

Gérard de Nerval
THE CHIMERAS
with an essay by Richard Holmes

János Pilinszky
CRATER: POEMS 1974–75

CONVERSATIONS WITH SHERYL SUTTON
with Éva Major

Nichita Stănescu
THE STILL UNBORN ABOUT THE DEAD
with Petru Popescu

THE SONG OF SONGS

A version by Peter Jay
Introduced by David Goldstein

ANVIL PRESS POETRY

First published in 1975
by Anvil Press Poetry Ltd
Neptune House 70 Royal Hill London SE10 8RF
New edition published in 1998

ISBN 0 85646 286 1

This book is published with financial assistance from
The Arts Council of England

A catalogue record for this book
is available from the British Library

Set in Monotype Bembo with Delphian figures
Printed and bound in England
by Redwood Books, Trowbridge, Wiltshire

INTRODUCTION

It is one of the ironies of literary history that had it not been for a rabbinical legalistic discussion and decision concerning the holy character of The Song of Songs one of the finest collections of sensual love-poetry might have been lost for ever. The discussion took place at Yavneh in the early second century AD. This was the famous centre of the Jewish academy which was established under the leadership of Rabban Jochanan ben Zakkai after the destruction of Jerusalem by the Romans in the year 70. The formidable task of the academy was to re-constitute Jewish life, and therefore also Jewish faith, after the political calamities that had overwhelmed it, and indeed were still to befall it. By this time the canon of Scripture had been almost completely established. The *Torah* (the Five Books of Moses) had been recognized as sacred for centuries, and the *Neviim* (the Prophets, i.e. Joshua to Malachi) had also been accorded canonicity. But there remained two books, now firmly implanted in the third division of the Hebrew Scriptures, the *Ketuvim* (Writings, Hagiographa), whose sacred character were still disputed, while others were definitely consigned to extra-canonical collections, such as the Apocrypha and the Pseudepigrapha.

The two books in dispute were Ecclesiastes (Hebrew title *Kohelet*) and The Song of Songs (*Shir ha-Shirim*). The discussion is recorded in the *Mishnah*, a large collection of legal arguments and decisions collected by Rabbi Judah ha-Nasi about 200 AD, but containing much early material, stretching back at least as far as the first century BC. It is Rabbi Akiva who emerges as the real champion of The Song of Songs, as will be seen from the passage in the tractate *Yadaim* (Hands) III, 5, part of the division *Toharot* (Cleannesses): 'All the Holy Scriptures defile the hands [i.e. are sufficiently sacred in character to require the hands to be in a particular state of ritual cleanliness]. The Song of Songs and Ecclesiastes defile the hands. Rabbi Judah says, The Song of Songs defiles the hands, but there is some dispute about Ecclesiastes. Rabbi Jose says, Ecclesiastes does not defile the hands, but there is some dispute about The Song of Songs. Rabbi Simeon says, Ecclesiastes is one of the things where the School of Shammai was more lenient than the School of Hillel [the opposite was usually the case, but in this instance, the School of Shammai did not consider Ecclesiastes sacred, and therefore the ritual requirements involved in touching the book were less severe]. Rabbi Simeon ben Azzai said, I have a tradition emanating from the seventy-two elders when Rabbi Eleazar ben Azariah was appointed [*c.* 100 AD] head of the academy that both The Song of Songs and Ecclesiastes defile the hands. Rabbi Akiva said, 'God forbid – no man in Israel has ever disputed the fact that The Song of Songs defiles the hands, for the whole world is not as worthy as the day on which The Song of Songs was given to Israel, for all the Writings are holy, but The Song of Songs is the Holy of Holies. If there was a dispute, it was only about Ecclesiastes. Rabbi Jochanan ben Joshua, Rabbi Akiva's brother-in-law, said, Both the dispute and the final decision were in accordance with the statement of Ben Azzai [i.e. both books were in dispute, and both were finally declared sacred].'

However, Rabbi Akiva's enthusiasm was not prompted by his appreciation of the sensual poetic beauty of the book. It was only because he was able to see its allegorical religious import that he defended its canonicity. It was in fact its very lack of direct spiritual meaning that put its status in jeopardy.

It contains no reference whatsoever to the life of faith, and the single mention of the name of God occurs in a metaphorical context (VIII.6; 26.3 in this translation). Similarly, Ecclesiastes was a doubtful addition to the canon because of its materialistic fatalism, and it was redeemed only through its closing verses which many scholars consider to have been written in, to correct the balance. Not that the literal beauty and significance of The Song of Songs went unnoticed. The many warnings by rabbinic authorities against taking the book at its face value show that such a literal reading was not uncommon, and that the temptation so to regard the book was ever-present. The improper use of The Song of Songs was much frowned upon. 'He who reads a verse from The Song of Songs, and turns it into an ordinary song, brings evil upon the world' (*Sanhedrin* 101a). 'He who trills his voice in reading The Song of Songs in a tavern, and turns it into an ordinary song has no share in the world to come' (*Tosefta Sanhedrin* 12, 10). At the same time great stress is laid on the extraordinary sanctity of the book. Once the book was accepted into the canon the rabbis went out of their way to defend its inclusion and the interpretation that they gave it. In a discussion of the words that may or may not be used in swearing an oath (*Shevuot* 35b) we read: 'Every mention of Solomon in The Song of Songs is holy — it is a song that belongs to the Sower of peace (*shalom*).' 'The Song of Songs was spoken by the Holy One, blessed be He. The choicest of all songs was spoken by the patriarchs, the righteous ones, the prophets, and the ministering angels' (*Midrash Zuta, Shir ha-Shirim*, 1). Solomon was able to write it only because 'the holy spirit rested upon him' (*Shir ha-Shirim Rabbah* 1, 8).

This adulation of the book derived from the rabbinic view that its subject-matter involved a love-story not between man and woman, but between God and His people

Israel. Practically every verse of the book can be, and was, interpreted in this way. The book, because it was divinely inspired, reflected historical events that were to take place long after Solomon's time, and it was a permanent reminder of the close relationship that existed between God and the Jewish people. In medieval times a further allegorical interpretation was added which saw The Song of Songs as a dialogue between the soul and the body, or between the human soul and the divine spirit, or between reason (or wisdom) and the senses. Thus Maimonides (d. 1204), the greatest of medieval Jewish philosophers, was able to lace his major work, *The Guide of the Perplexed*, with many quotations from The Song of Songs, despite his extremely puritanical attitude towards human sexual emotion and experience, even within marriage.

Similarly, Christianity, which inherited the book from the Synagogue, imposed its allegorical pattern, seeing it as portraying the relationship between Christ and his Church. It also adopted a parallel philosophical interpretation in the Middle Ages, and both Jewish and Christian mystics seized upon the erotic imagery as a profound symbolic expression of the yearning of the soul for union with its source in God.

And yet, despite these layers upon layers of imposed interpretation, the literary poetic beauty of the book consistently re-asserted itself. The effect of its erotic lyricism was suppressed for a time, but could not be subdued, and its influence comes to the surface again in the Latin poems of Western Christendom, and the Hebrew poems of the Jews of Spain.

The origin and nature of the book have been the subject of scholarly controversy for centuries. One cannot do better when approaching these problems than to start one's investigation with the text itself, bearing in mind that the traditional versification and chapter-divisions, as in all biblical books, were later additions to the Hebrew text. It is difficult to discover any logically consistent narrative thread in the book. Certainly the 'story-line', if there is one, is not the most striking or the most remarkable element. Indeed, it is this lack of a clear story that has caused so many different interpretations to be placed upon the work. Its chief feature is that of a lyrical love-poem, or of a collection of love-poems. Sometimes the speaker is a man, sometimes a woman and sometimes a third person. The background varies. We move from a pastoral to an urban environment and then back again to the country. There are refrains that recur throughout the book. Geographical locations are also of a varied character, most of them being in Northern Israel, such as Hermon and Senir, while a few are to be found to the centre or the south of the country, such as Jerusalem and En-Gedi. The language of the book also has diverse characteristics. Scholars have detected both Greek and Persian influences in the Hebrew vocabulary, which would point to a fairly late date. There are certain 'Aramaisms' too, which at first were also considered to indicate a late date, but which have now been shown to be characteristic of Hebrew and cognate languages emanating from an earlier period. There are a considerable number of difficult verbal forms, and the vocabulary too is far from simple, since it contains Hebrew words which are found nowhere else in the biblical literature. The authorship of the book is ascribed at the very beginning to Solomon (tenth century BC), and his name occurs six times elsewhere in the book. It is fair to deduce, therefore, that there was an association of some kind with Solomon – that the book was read in his court, or that he wrote all or part of it, or that it was a particular favourite of his, or that it was compiled in his honour, or that because he was renowned for both his verbal wisdom and his amorous adventures the book makes frequent mention of him, and was later ascribed to him. Because the book cannot be definitely assigned to one author, or to one geographical locality, or to one specific date, the most natural tentative conclusion is to assume that it is a collection of love-poems, some longer, some shorter, which were composed over a considerable period of time, perhaps from the eighth to the third centuries BC, either in the northern or southern kingdom, or both. The question of date and authorship is further complicated by the fact that we are here dealing to a large extent with oral transmission. The lyrics would be spoken, or, more probably, sung, and would be handed down from one generation to another, and therefore prone to alteration, addition, expansion and contraction. We have no way of telling when the book reached its present form, except that it must have been very much as it is today by the second century BC, when the question of canonicity began to arise.

This portrayal of the book is, of course, vague and therefore unsatisfactory, but a consideration of the text itself gives the reader no clearer or more definite lead to follow. Other interpretations have been imposed, with varying degrees of justification, from without.

It has been regarded, for example, as a drama, with a chorus of maidens, and three principal characters, King Solomon, a country-girl and her country lover.

The action revolves round the attempt of the king to inveigle the girl into his harem, despite her protests and those of her true lover. True love at last wins through, and the king's efforts come to naught. Another view would have it that we are here dealing with a cult ritual, connected with pagan customs celebrated at a spring festival, and that the book contains hymns and lyrics relevant to a fertility-cult, or to the resurrection in the spring of the god Tammuz–Adonis. A third interpretation sees it as a collection of wedding-songs, perhaps associated with a marriage of King Solomon himself, and no doubt accompanied by choric dancing.

All these theories are in their own way ingenious, but they all suffer from their determined attempt to impose a unified pattern on the book as a whole. And a pattern is simply not there. It is preferable to consider the poems as they are, taking note only of the sex of the speaker, which is usually easily discernible from the gender of the speech-forms. The actual lines of division between one poem and another may be disputed. It is the only interpretative addition we have made. In this we have followed Robert Gordis's text, where each poem seems to us to stand on its own as a complete unit.

This is not the place to describe at length the nature of biblical Hebrew poetry except to point out that in the Song of Moses (Exodus 15) and the Song of Deborah (Judges 5) we have probably the oldest strata of that literature. But there is very little which in either style or content is comparable to The Song of Songs. Lyrical love-poetry by its very nature is not likely to occur often in a collection of books which have for the most part history, ritual, law, ethics and theology as their main themes. However there are one or two pointers to the fact that The Song of Songs was written within an accepted poetic convention whose imagery was not altogether uncommon. The Book of Proverbs describes the ways of the harlot, and portrays her enticements as follows:

> ... I have come out to meet you,
> to watch for you and find you.
> I have spread coverings on my bed
> of coloured linen from Egypt.

> *I have sprinkled my bed with myrrh,*
> *my clothes with aloes and cassia.*
> *Come! Let us drown ourselves in pleasure,*
> *let us spend a whole night of love.*
>
> (7.15–18; NEB)

This is contrasted with the faithful love of the true wife:

> *May your fountain be blessed.*
> *May you enjoy the wife of your youth.*
> *A hind of love, a graceful doe,*
> *May her breasts satisfy you always.*
> *May you be constantly overwhelmed with her love.*
>
> (5.18–19)

Or consider this glorious future forecast for Israel by Hosea:

> *He shall blossom as the lily,*
> *And cast forth his roots as Lebanon.*
> *His branches shall spread*
> *And his beauty shall be as the olive-tree,*
> *And his fragrance as Lebanon.*
> *They that dwell under his shadow shall again*
> *Make corn to grow,*
> *And shall blossom as the vine.*
> *The scent thereof shall be as the wine of Lebanon.*
>
> (14.6–8; JPSA)

The descriptions of behemoth and leviathan in Job, 40 and 41, although different obviously in content, are similar in style to the eulogies of the lovers in The Song of Songs, in the way that each part of their anatomy is matched by a powerful metaphor.

His tail is rigid as a cedar,
the sinews of his flanks are closely knit,
his bones are tubes of bronze,
and his limbs like bars of iron.
(40.17–18; NEB)

His back is row upon row of shields,
enclosed in a wall of flints...
his nostrils pour forth smoke
like a cauldron...
His breath sets burning coals ablaze...
His heart is firm as a rock...
(41.15, 20–21, 24; NEB)

But we do not have to limit ourselves to biblical literature in our search for stylistic parallels to The Song of Songs. The literature of the ancient Near East in general can afford us much enlightening material. A collection of Egyptian love-lyrics is particularly relevant here. In this collection the lovers are referred to as 'brother and sister', which has an important bearing on the use of these terms in the biblical collection.

Would that thou wouldst come (to the sister speedily),
Like a horse of the king,
Picked from a thousand of all steeds,
The foremost of the stables.

(Pritchard, 468a)

This comparison of the beloved to a royal steed is also found in our collection: 'I shall compare you, my love, to a mare among Pharaoh's chariot-horses' (i.9). And the physical sickness induced by love (ii.5 and v.8) was also expressed by the Egyptian poet:

> *Seven (days) to yesterday I have not seen the sister,*
> *And a sickness has invaded me.*
> *My body has become heavy,*
> *Forgetful of my own self.*
>
> (Pritchard, 468b)

The voice of the bird announcing the spring (ii.12–13) is paralleled by

> *The voice of the swallow speaks and says:*
> *'The land has brightened – what is thy need?'*
>
> (Pritchard, 468a)

These Egyptian love-songs, however, are considerably earlier than our collection, dating from the later Egyptian Empire (1300–1100 BC). An even earlier poem of ritualistic significance is a Sumerian love-song from about 2000 BC, and it contains a couplet whose imagery is not dissimilar to that of The Song of Songs:

> *O my god, of the wine-maid, sweet is her date-wine,*
> *Like her date-wine, sweet is her vulva, sweet is her date-wine ...*
>
> (Pritchard, 496b)

A Sumerian hymn to the goddess Ishtar (Pritchard 383) also exhibits parallels with the praise of the beloved in our text. Parallels could also be drawn from classical Greek literature, and there is considerable evidence that knowledge and experience of Hellenic and Hellenistic culture among Jews was more widespread than commonly thought. The researches of Saul Lieberman, in particular (*Greek in Jewish Palestine*, New York, 1942, and *Hellenism in Jewish Palestine*, New York, 1950), have extended our knowledge of this aspect of the influence on Jews and Judaism of other civilizations. We also know that several warnings were issued by the rabbinic authorities against the learning of Greek, because in their view it might have led to the imitation of pagan religious rituals, and atheistic philosophical ideas. These warnings would not have been issued had they not been prompted by a desire on the part of some Jews to familiarize themselves with the Greek creative genius. Indeed, in *Sotah* 49b we read that, in the house of Rabban Simeon b. Gamliel's father, five hundred children were taught Torah, and five hundred were taught Greek. This, however, was no doubt an exceptional case prompted by the relationship of the patriarch with the government. In any event, rabbinic source-material relating to Greek is relevant only if we posit a very late date for the composition of The Song of Songs. More cogent is the indisputable fact that Greek manners and culture deeply influenced the Hashmonean dynasty from the middle of the second century BC onwards.

Whenever literary parallels are drawn, however, we must try to distinguish between direct cross-influence on the one hand, and, on the other, the natural resemblance in content, and perhaps also in style, of the work of a number of poets dealing with the same subject-matter. The amount of material we have to deal with is comparatively scanty, and therefore it would be rash to do more than to point out similarities, without deducing from them definite conclusions.

But we may be forgiven if we see The Song of Songs as the tip of an iceberg (if that is not too inappropriate a simile), the larger proportion of which is hidden from our sight. It is a tantalizing thought that at some time, somewhere, in ancient Palestine, love poems of the calibre of The Song of Songs were written, perhaps in great numbers, and that they may be discovered again one day, like the scrolls from the Dead Sea.

David Goldstein

TRANSLATOR'S PREFACE

Chance led me in 1966 to Robert Gordis's edition of The Song of Songs. I had been excited at recognizing striking similarities to the Hebrew, which I then knew only in the Authorized Version, in *Love Poems of Ancient Egypt* (translated by Ezra Pound and Noel Stock; New Directions, New York, 1961). Gordis's commentary confirmed my suspicion that The Song of Songs was not entirely what it seemed to be in the Bible's presentation. 'If The Song of Songs be approached without any preconceptions,' he wrote, 'it reveals itself as a collection of lyrics.'

It seemed extraordinary that a collection of poems of this acknowledged stature – the total remnants of ancient Hebrew secular poetry – could still be popularly misrepresented. I undertook this version, using at first what commentaries and other translations I could find, despite knowing no Hebrew. I tried to realize the poems in terms that would align them with the similar poetry of other early near-eastern cultures, the Pound and Stock translations being for this purpose both a model and a point of reference.

Evidence is scant, but it cannot be wholly fanciful to suppose that these poems, or other similar songs from the same parts, were known to the Greek Alexandrian world. It would be unjustified to draw more than the most tentative conclusions from what may be casual parallels, especially in view of the destruction of so much of the literature of the ancient Egyptians, Hebrews and Alexandrian Greeks. But Alexandria, with its great library and scholar-poets, could have been an important point of contact between these cultures in the third and second centuries BC. That there were strong connections in trade and culture between Palestine and the Greek world long before the Roman intervention is well known. Two important Greek poets were natives of Gadara, a few miles to the south of Galilee – Meleager (*c.* 140–70 BC), whose *Garland*, an anthology of Greek epigrams, has given us most of the Alexandrian poetry preserved in *The Greek Anthology*; and his younger contemporary, the philosopher and poet Philodemos (*c.* 110–40 BC), who emigrated to Rome about 75 BC.

Meleager's beautiful description of spring (*Palatine Anthology* 9.360) is notably un-Greek in sentiment, and may owe something both to the literary tradition and the scenery of his homeland. An anonymous Greek epigram (*Pal. Anth.* 5.305) – unusual because, like Meleager's poem, it is in hexameters, the metre of pastoral poetry, not elegiac couplets which are the standard form for epigram – suggests that eroticism similar to that of The Song of Songs may have been more prevalent in lost Alexandrian pastoral poetry than we can now judge. The style is similar to that of Bion, the pastoral poet who wrote the famous lament for Adonis (*c.* 100 BC):

> *Yesterday evening a girl kissed me with moist lips,*
> *the kiss was nectar, her mouth exhaled nectar*
> *and I am drunk on the kiss*
> *I have drunk deep of love.*

Theokritos has occasionally been cited as an analogous poet, and indeed some of the poems of The Song of Songs may have been written as late as his lifetime (*c.* 310–250 BC). The evidence for any plausible connection is thin, though Theokritos's pastoral world seems to show slight traces of Syrian material. After leaving Syracuse, where he wrote his earliest poems, he lived in Alexandria and Kos. Resemblances to The Song of Songs seem more than casual only in the song set in Ptolemy's court at the Festival of Adonis, which the two Alexandrian housewives, Praxinoa and Gorgo, go to hear: 'Goddess of many names and temples, Bereniké's daughter Arsinoë, lovely as Helen, pampers Adonis with all good things to please you. Beside him lie all the best things from trees in their ripeness, tender fruits kept in silver baskets, gold casks of Syrian perfumes; all cakes which women shape in baking-tins, mixing blossoms of every kind with white flour, from sweet honey to liquid oil, all are there, shaped like bird or beast.'

Roman poets developed the erotic elegy considerably. With little indigenous lyric or pastoral poetry to turn to, they looked to the Alexandrians, and the early Greek lyric poets, for themes and forms. In poets like Catullus and Tibullus we find the convention of the serenade of the shut-out lover employed; in The Song of Songs, poem 17, the girl who has shut out her lover speaks. It isn't hard to imagine lost Greek poems in which the convention was used. But more important than this sort of conjecture is the fact that the Hebrew poem displays the same sort of sophisticated irony and conscious dramatic use of traditional poetic modes, which we associate with such cosmopolitan poets as Propertius – the most Alexandrian of the Roman poets.

These considerations are only marginally relevant to the poetry; and perhaps more relevant to my general approach as an interpreter than to the Hebrew poems themselves. I give them because the poems otherwise seem to exist in a cultural limbo. Far the most important literary parallel to the Hebrew poems, I believe, is the early Egyptian poetry. There is much common ground between the two in imagery and symbolism, style and attitudes. My own stylistic debt to Pound's Egyptian translation *Conversations in Courtship* is too obvious to need emphasizing, as all who know that beautiful poem will recognize:

> *Darling, you only, there is no duplicate,*
> *More lovely than all other womanhood,*
> > *luminous, perfect,*
> *A star coming over the sky-line at new year,*
> > *a good year,*
> *Splendid in colors,*
> > *with allure in the eye's turn ...*

There is little that needs explanation in the poems. The notes record some points which the reader may feel need attention. The poems take the form of dramatic lyrics, spoken either by a man or a woman: I take them to be impersonal poems, rather than direct addresses by the poet to his audience. A few are duets, and I assign speakers to these. We must imagine that many of the poems were songs, perhaps – like our ballads – altered and added to over the centuries. Some of the poems (notably 17) are clearly works of more conscious 'literature'. The earliest datable poem is of the tenth century, but some of the traditional material may be earlier. I would guess that the latest poems might have been composed in the fourth century. The characteristic symbolism of the poems, as of other 'primitive' poetry such as the Aztec, is often condensed, subtle and complex. It is the natural language of erotic lyrical poetry. (The point does not need labouring that the poems are rife with nature imagery – flowers, fruit, spices, etc. – which carry both literal and sexual-symbolic significance.) Poem 7 gives a good example of such a complex of both literal and symbolic meaning – 'Bring me raisin-cakes, support me with apples.' The girl's response in

19

poem 27 to her brothers' plans for her betrothal sums up her feelings in symbolic terms which have the concision of epigram.

The modern reader may have some difficulty in adjusting to aesthetic standards of beauty, such as comparisons of women with mares, of a girl's hair to the appearance of a herd of goats on a mountain-side, and so on. More than 2,000 years ago these would have been compliments suggestive of natural wealth, in an age which did not divorce man from the environment, the spirit from the body, nor sexual from natural beauty.

To Robert Gordis's excellent work I must make the fullest acknowledgment of gratitude. The division of the poems and many points of interpretation – the most important of which are recorded in the notes – have been adopted from his edition.

When in 1969 I came to revise the translations, I was fortunate to have the help of Dr David Goldstein. I owe him a special debt of thanks both for his generous help in working over the poems with me, correcting and improving my drafts; and for undertaking the Introduction to the book, and supplying a bibliography. My own instincts must be blamed for any erratic solutions to the textual problems, and all quirks of interpretation which I have allowed to override his sympathetic judgment. I am grateful also to Stanley Moss for a large number of critical suggestions which have helped in the final revision of the poems.

I have retained the traditional title of the collection, though it is a misnomer, for familiarity's sake. References to chapter and verse of the biblical text for each poem are given at the end of the book.

Peter Jay

THE SONG OF SONGS

which is Solomon's

1

Let him give me his kisses to drink!
Your love-making is better than wine
because of your perfumes' presence,
your presence, oil poured out –
no wonder all the girls love you.

Draw me in after you, we will hurry.
– The king has brought me into his rooms...
I will be happy in you, inhaling
your love-making rather than wine –
your manliness, for which all the girls love you.

2

I am dark, daughters of Jerusalem – yet beautiful
as the tents of Kedar, or Solomon's tapestry.
Don't stare at me because I am tanned,
because the sun has stared at me;
my brothers were angry with me
and made me look after their vineyards,
but I neglected my own.

3

Tell me, love of my soul, where you graze your
    sheep
and where you rest them at noon?
Why should I sit here, like a nomad
among your companions' flocks,
                        and the men saying
'If you don't know where, my beauty, try
the sheep-tracks – take your goats off to graze
by the shepherds' tents.'

4

A MAN

I shall compare you, my love, to a mare
        among Pharaoh's chariot-horses,
your cheeks framed perfectly with braid
a string of beads circling your throat –
we will make you gold loops
        pinpointed with silver.

A WOMAN

While the king lies on his couch, my spikenard
breathes out its fragrance. My love
is a bundle of myrrh
        lying between my breasts,
a cluster of henna blossom
        from En-Gedi's vineyards.

5

A MAN

Yes, you are fair, my love
fair, with a dove's eyes.

A WOMAN

Love, you are handsome, handsome, my love
– our bed is green.

BOTH

The beams of our house are cedars
our rafters, the branches of fir trees.

6

A WOMAN

I am a plain crocus
a windflower in the valley.

A MAN

A windflower found among thorns
is my love among the young women.

A WOMAN

Among the young men my lover is like
an apple tree among the trees of a wood.
In its shadow I rest happily,
its fruit, sweet to my taste.

7

Under the sign of his love
he has brought me to the tavern.
Bring me raisin-cakes,
                    support me with apples,
I feel so faint with love –

his left hand under my head,
his right, holding me close –

By the gazelles and deer of the field
I make you swear, daughters of Jerusalem,
not to disturb or interrupt our love
till it is satisfied.

8

Listen – my lover! He comes bounding
over the mountains, leaping the hills –
he is like a gazelle, he is like
a young stag.

        Now he stands
behind our wall, peering
through the windows and lattice, saying

'Up, my love, come away! Winter is past
the rains are over and gone,
        flowers appear on the earth,
the time for singing has come, you can hear
the turtle-dove's song in our land.
Green figs on the fig tree
        the blossoming vines are fragrant,
up, my love, my beauty, and come away.'

9

A MAN

By the cracked rocks, my dove, in the shadow of
   the cliff may I
see your face – let me hear your voice –
sweet is your voice, and your face full of beauty –

A WOMAN

Catch the jackals, little
jackals that raid the vineyards –
just when ours is in blossom.

10

My love is mine, I am his –
he grazes among the anemones.
Until day breathes
        and the shadows are gone
turn, my love, and be like
a gazelle or a young stag
climbing the Cleft Mountains.

11

Nights on my bed I searched for the man
        my soul loves – I
searched, but did not find him.
'I will get up and go round the town
        through the streets and squares
and hunt out the man I love.'

I looked, but could not find him.

Soldiers making their rounds in the town met me
('Have you seen the man I love?')
and I'd scarcely passed them when
        I finally found him.
I held him, I wouldn't let go
till I had brought him back
        to mother's house
to the room of the woman who bore me.

By the gazelles and deer of the field
I make you swear, daughters of Jerusalem,
not to disturb or interrupt our love
till it is satisfied.

12

What is this coming out of the desert
                    like columns of smoke?
thick with myrrh and frankincense
and all the spices a merchant could sell?
                    It is Solomon's litter,
sixty men, Israel's bravest around it
all of them swordsmen, trained warriors.
Each has a sword at his thigh
to combat the terrors of darkness.

King Solomon built himself a carriage
of Lebanon timber; he made it with silver posts,
with gold, and seats dyed in murex, inlays
lovingly placed inside
                    by Jerusalem's daughters.
Come out, daughters of Zion – gaze at King Solomon,
at the crown his mother crowned him with
                    on the day of his wedding,
the day of his gladness of heart.

13

Love, you are beautiful,
    fair, my love,
through your veil your eyes are like doves' eyes,
your hair sweeps down
    as a herd of goats trailing down Gilead,
your teeth are like lambs ready for shearing
    coming out of the dip,
each partnered with a twin.
Your lips are a scarlet thread,
    the cut of your mouth is perfect.
Under the veil your temples
    shine like a pomegranate-slice,
your neck is like David's tower
    built as a landmark,
a thousand shields hanging on it
    and all the armour of heroes.
And your breasts – two fawns,
    a gazelle's twins,
grazing among the anemones.
Until day breathes
    and the shadows are gone
I will go down
    to the mountain of myrrh
the frankincense hill.
    You are all fair, my love
you are flawless.

14

From Lebanon with me, my bride, with me from
    Lebanon
you shall come:
                    Come from Amana's peak
the summits of Senir and Hermon
from the lion-dens
                    from the leopard-mountains.

15

With one sign from those eyes
the flash of one gem on your necklace
you have taken my heart. Sister my bride,
how delightful your love-making is,
how much better than wine
and the scent of your perfumes than all spices...

Your lips, my bride, dripping honey
honey and milk are under your tongue
and the smell of your clothes is like the smell of
    Lebanon.

16

A MAN

A locked garden is my sister, my bride
a closed spring, a sealed fountain.
Your branches are a pomegranate orchard
with all precious fruits, henna and roses
saffron and spikenard, cassia, cinnamon,
with frankincense trees, myrrh and aloes,
all perfect spices...

A WOMAN

My garden's fountain is a well
of living waters streaming from Lebanon...
Awake, North Wind – South, advance –
breathe on my garden, let its fragrance flow out
enticing my lover into his garden
to taste its precious fruit.

A MAN

I have come into my garden
sister, my bride

I am gathering myrrh and spices
licking the honey from the comb
drinking the wine and milk.

A WOMAN

Eat, my friend, drink –
lover, be drunk with love.

17

I was drowsy, but my heart was awake. Listen!
My lover beats at the door.
      'Sister my love,
open and let me in
      my dove, my perfection,
my head is soaked with dew
      hair drenched with drops of the night.'
– 'I am already undressed,
      why should I get dressed again,
I've washed my feet
      and why should I get them dirty?'

He took his hand off the bolted door
      and my heart sank...
I got up to let him in,
my hands sticky with myrrh, fingers
dripping myrrh on the latch
      and flung the door open –
but he was gone in the darkness.
My heart longed for his voice;
I looked, but did not find him,
called, but he gave no reply.
Soldiers making their rounds in the city
found me, and beat me up,
those Wall-Guards stripped off my coat...

I make you swear, daughters of Jerusalem
if you find my lover, tell him
how sick I am with love.

(And what's your lover
    more than anyone else's,
darling?
    Why so special
for you to make us promise?)

He has a sparkling appearance –
you'd pick him out of ten thousand.
His face is the purest gold, his hair
a heap of curls, black as a raven.
His eyes float like doves in a pool
suspended, bathing in milk.
His cheeks smell like fragrant spice-beds,
his lips are anemones
        overflowing with myrrh,
his hands gold clasps set in topaz,
an ivory cask his body, lapis-lazuli-veined,
pillars of marble on gold bases – his legs:
the sight of him is like Lebanon,
        grand as the cedars,
his talking, sweetness itself,
        he is altogether delightful.
Daughters of Jerusalem –
        this is my lover and friend.

(But darling, where can he have got to?
Tell us which way he went,
so we can find him with you.)

My lover has gone
            down to his garden
into his spice-beds
            to feed there in the orchards
picking anemones...

I am my lover's, and he is mine
as he grazes among the anemones.

18

O my love, you are fair as Tirzah
beautiful as Jerusalem
awesome as all the great sights!

Turn your eyes away, they torment me...

Your hair sweeps down
        as a herd of goats trailing down Gilead,
your teeth are like lambs ready for shearing
        coming out of the dip,
each partnered with a twin.
Under the veil your temples
        shine like a pomegranate-slice.

19

There are sixty queens, eighty mistresses and
    countless other young women,
my dove, my perfection is One –
her mother's darling, matchless to the woman who
    bore her.
The young women looked
          and said how lucky she was,
even the queens and mistresses saw
          and praised her.

20

Who is she gazing out
        like the dawn star
clear as the moon
        pure as the sun
awesome as all the great sights?

I went down to the nut orchard
to look at the shoots in the valley, to see
whether the vine was in bud
        and the pomegranate blooming.
Ecstasy: for there,
        O my nobleman's daughter,
you will give me your myrrh.

21

THE MEN

Turn, turn again, Shulemite
turn, let us see you again!

THE WOMAN

What can you see in me,
            a mere girl from Shulem –
a whole chorus of dancers?

THE MEN

How graceful your steps in sandals,
            nobleman's daughter...
the curves of your thighs are like jewels
            shaped by a master craftsman,
your vulva a rounded cup
            never failing in wine.
Your belly slopes like a heap of grain,
            ringed with anemones,
your breasts are like two fawns,
            a gazelle's twins,

your neck an ivory tower,
        your eyes
like the pools in Heshbon
        by the gate of Bath-rabbim.
Your nose is like Lebanon's tower
        facing Damascus.
Like Carmel your head,
        lustrous the thread of your hair —
a king is trapped in your locks!

22

How beautiful, what a joy, my love!
Like a palm tree you stand,
your breasts, its bunches of dates.
                              I said
'I will climb up this palm tree
          clasping its branches.
And your breasts will be like vine–clusters
the scent of your breath like apples,
for your kiss is like the best wine
          which arouses lovers,
stirring the sleeping lips with desire.'

23

I am my lover's, his desire is for me.
Come, my love, let us go to the country,
stay in a village, get up early, go
down to the vineyards to see
whether the vines are in bud
                    the grape-blossom open
and the pomegranate blooming...

There I will give you my love.

Mandrakes breathe out their fragrance.
By our doors you will find
all the fruit, new and old, my love
which I have stored for you.

24

If only you were my brother
        fed at my mother's breast!
Then I'd meet you outside
        kiss you
– no one would be shocked –
        I'd take you
bring you to mother's house,
        mother who taught me,
give you spiced wine to drink,
        my pomegranate-wine –

his left hand under my head,
his right, holding me close –

And I would exclaim:
I make you swear, daughters of Jerusalem,
not to disturb or interrupt our love
till it is satisfied.

25

– Who is this coming out of the desert,
clinging to her lover?

– Under the apple tree I woke you.
There your mother laboured for you,
laboured and gave you life.

26

Keep me as a seal on your heart,
    a seal on your arm –
for lust is stubborn as death
    pitiless as the grave,
its glowing coals
    burn with the fiercest flames.
Floods cannot wash desire away
    nor rivers put it out.
If a man offered
    all the wealth of his house
for love –
    he would be utterly scorned.

27

THE BROTHERS

We have a little sister
      and she has no breasts.
What shall we do with our sister
when her time comes to be courted?
If she is a wall
      we will fortify her with silver,
a gate — we will board her up
      with planks of cedar.

THE GIRL

I am a wall, my breasts
      will be like its towers.
In my lover's eyes I will be
      the one who brings peace.

28

Solomon had a vineyard at Baal-hamon
which he let out to tenants.
For its fruit you would pay
a thousand pieces of silver.
My vineyard, my very own, lies before me:
Solomon, keep your thousands
and your tenants their twenty per cent!

29

O my love, as you sit in the garden, your
    companions
listen alert to your voice;
now let me hear it, saying

'Lose no time, my love; be like
a gazelle or a young stag
climbing the mountains of spices.

NOTES

Title This, and the ascription to Solomon, were presumably added by an editor who accepted the popular theory of Solomon's authorship (he was also credited with writing Proverbs and Ecclesiastes).

1 The change of person between lines 1 and 2 is a Hebrew idiom. Unless the poem is the girl's dream of a royal marriage, *king* stands for 'bridegroom' (a common West-Semitic and Jewish usage – Gordis).

2 *Daughters of Jerusalem* The term means simply 'women of Jerusalem'.
Kedar The name of a nomadic tribe in the desert areas of the north of Saudi-Arabia.
Solomon's tapestry A generic term like Louis XIV furniture, etc.

3 The poem could also be taken as a duet between the girl and the men, in question and answer form. I have added 'and the men saying' to clarify what I take to be an imagined answer.

4 En-Gedi, on the western shore of the Dead Sea, was famous for its vineyards. The name may mean 'spring of the kid'.

5 A tryst-song of northern origin, to judge by the trees mentioned.

6 The Authorized Version's famous 'rose of Sharon' was nothing so glamorous; the girl says she is 'a crocus of Sharon', the coastal plain stretching from Jaffa to Caesarea.

7 The formulaic adjuration (literally 'not to arouse nor waken our love / till love is ready'), which occurs also in poems 11 and 24, can be taken in two ways; either to mean 'let us make love in our own good time', or as Gordis suggests, as a request not to interrupt the lovers, till they are ready to be disturbed – i.e. have satisfied their love. Sense favours the latter, though the translation is interpretative rather than literal.

9   A cryptic piece; perhaps fragmentary.

10   *Cleft Mountains* The Hebrew phrase means either 'divided (or dividing) mountains', or 'mountains of Bether' – south-west of Jerusalem.

12   Gordis notes here the only specifically national reference to Israel in the book. If the poem was composed for a marriage of Solomon to a foreign, perhaps Egyptian, princess it would be the book's oldest datable poem, of the tenth century BC.
     Lebanon Here as elsewhere in the poems this refers to the mountain range.

13   Parts of this straightforward *wasf* (praise poem) are clearly formulaic; cf. poem 18, and for 'Until day breathes...' poem 10.
     Gilead Here of a particular mountain in the hill-country east of the river Jordan and north-west of the modern Amman.
     David's tower Nothing is known of this.

14   Perhaps a fragment of a song from the northern mountains; *Amana* and *Senir* are probably peaks of the Anti-Lebanon range, of which Hermon is the southernmost peak.

16   This poem is not older than the Persian period, sixth century BC, if the evidence of a Persian word is to be trusted (Gordis). The last two lines either form a rare, though not unparalleled usage of the plural for singular (literally 'Eat, my friends,... lovers, be drunk...'); or could be taken as the poet's final comment, and not a part of the dialogue.

17   The longest and most sophisticated poem in the collection – perhaps therefore one of the latest in date – takes the form of a dream, with traditional poetic elements (the *wasf* in praise of the lover, the closing description of love) subtly and dramatically incorporated. Poem 11 is a shorter variation. For its metrical variety, see Gordis, whose view that the *wasf* praises the lover's health and virility as well as good looks is supported by his quotation of this Babylonian charm –

    Like lapis-lazuli I want to cleanse his body
    Like marble his features should shine

> *Like pure silver, like red gold*
> *I want to make clean what is dull.*

The comments made by the daughters of Jerusalem are best taken as being imagined by the girl in her dream. Breaking the poem up into a narrative with speakers, as is sometimes done, destroys its dramatic force as well as its dream-logic.

darling Literally 'fairest among women'.

18   *Tirzah* West of the river Jordan, this city was capital of the Northern Kingdom until 887 BC. As Jerusalem was capital of the Southern Kingdom at this time, the comparisons gain point, as Gordis suggests, if the poem was written while Tirzah was still a capital.

awesome as all the great sights A famous crux: 'The traditional rendering 'terrible as an army with banners' is hardly satisfactory' (Gordis, whose interpretation I follow).

20   For the last three lines of the translation, I follow Gordis's interpretation of Tur-Sinai's emendation.

21   Possibly a marriage-dance, along the lines of the sword-dance performed by Syrian brides, is being described. There is no agreement on the meaning of the phrase which I translate as 'A whole chorus of dancers?' Literally it is 'as in the dance of Mahanaim [or, of two companies]'. Gordis takes the phrase as the men's response to her question, and translates 'Indeed, the counter-dance.' Mahanaim was a village near Mt Gilead.

Shulem Not far south-west of the Sea of Galilee (perhaps to be identified with Shunem).

Heshbon Modern Hisban, about twenty miles south-west of Amman.

Bath-rabbim Probably a place-name; it could mean 'the populous city'.

Damascus Just east of Mt Hermon.

Carmel Literally 'the purple land'; the coastal mountain just south of Haifa.

25   Another cryptic, possibly fragmentary, poem.

fiercest flames Literally 'God's flames', a Hebrew mode of expressing the superlative.

26   The alternative explanation of this poem, which Gordis adopts, gives the first section to the girl's suitors. It would then describe the gifts they plan to offer for her hand (silver and cedar symbolizing expensive gifts), and at the same time their strategy of 'invasion' of the girl (the silver and cedar would then symbolize *offensive* siege-weapons – tower and battering-ram). Gordis translates the crucial section as

> *If she be a wall,*
> *We will build a turret of silver against her;*
> *If she be a gate,*
> *We will besiege her with boards of cedar.*

Wall and *gate* are not contrasted, but rather parallel, in this reading of the poem.

    Giving the lines to her brothers, and taking the *wall* and *gate* as contrasted is the traditional interpretation, and on this occasion the most effective. The sense is: if she is a wall (refuses overtures, or is difficult to marry off), we'll make an attractive proposition of her by giving a good dowry; but if she's a gate (too compliant) we'll keep suitors at bay.

    It strikes me as more probable that the girl's brothers would feel she is too young to marry, than her suitors. The girl's answer suggests that there is a distinction between *wall* and *gate*, since she only says that she is a wall. As an argument from her silence this cannot be conclusive; but Hebrew generally likes to maintain parallelisms.

    The future tenses of the last sentence are mine: Hebrew does not distinguish between present and future.

28   *Baal-hamon* Otherwise unknown, unless it is a mistake for Baal Hermon. Gordis suggests that it is an imaginary place-name with the sense 'master of wealth', which is apt for the context.

BIBLIOGRAPHY

TRANSLATIONS

Bible, Authorized and Revised Versions
The Holy Scriptures, Jewish Publication Society of America, 1917
The Jerusalem Bible, 1965
The Five Megillot and Jonah. A New Translation, Jewish Publication
    Society of America, 1969
The New English Bible, 1970

Falk, Marcia, *The Song of Songs*, New York, 1977
Gordis, Robert, *The Song of Songs: A Study, Modern Translation and
    Commentary*, New York, 1954
Moffatt, James, *A New Translation of the Bible*, New York, 1935
Powis Smith and Goodspeed, eds., *The Bible, An American Translation*
    (The Song of Songs translated by T. J. Meek), Chicago, 1923
Schonfield, Hugh, *The Song of Songs*, New York, 1960

BACKGROUND LITERATURE

Erman, A., *The Literature of the Ancient Egyptians*, New York, 1927
Lambert, W. G., *Babylonian Wisdom Literature*, Oxford, 1960
Pritchard, J. B., *Ancient Near Eastern Texts Relating to the Old
    Testament*, Princeton, 1950

BIBLICAL LITERATURE

Driver, S. R., *Introduction to the Literature of the Old Testament*, 1897
Margolis, M. L., *The Hebrew Scriptures in the Making*, Philadelphia,
    1922

Pfeiffer, R. H., *Introduction to the Old Testament*, 1952
Rowley, H. H., *The Growth of the Old Testament*, 1950
Sandmel, S., *The Hebrew Scriptures*, New York, 1963

STUDIES OF THE SONG OF SONGS

Albright, W. F., 'Archaic Survivals in the Text of Canticles', *Hebrew and Semitic Studies Presented to G. R. Driver*, Oxford, 1963
Gaster, T. H., 'The Song of Songs', *Commentary*, vol. 13 (April 1952)
Gordis, R., 'A Wedding Song for Solomon', *Journal of Biblical Literature*, vol. 63 (1944)
Lehrman, S. M., 'The Song of Songs: Introduction and Commentary', *The Five Megilloth*, Soncino Press, 1946
Meek, T. J., 'Canticles and the Tammuz Cult', *American Journal of Semitic Languages*, vol. 48 (1930)
Meek, T. J., 'Babylonian Parallels to The Song of Songs', *Journal of Biblical Literature*, vol. 43 (1923)
Rowley, H. H., 'The Interpretation of The Song of Songs', *Journal of Theological Studies*, vol. 38 (1937)
Rowley, H. H., 'The Song of Songs – An Examination of Recent Theory', *Journal of the Royal Asiatic Society*, 1938
Rowley, H. H., 'The Meaning of the Shulammite', *American Journal of Semitic Languages*, vol. 56 (1939)
Schmidt, N., 'Is Canticles an Adonis Liturgy?', *Journal of the American Oriental Society*, vol. 46 (1926)
Schoff, W. H., ed. *The Song of Songs – A Symposium*, Philadelphia, 1924
Stephan, St. H., *Modern Palestinian Parallels to The Song of Songs*, Jerusalem, 1926
Waterman, L., 'The Role of Solomon in The Song of Songs', *Journal of Biblical Literature*, vol. 56 (1936)
Waterman, L., *The Song of Songs Interpreted as a Dramatic Poem*, Ann Arbor, 1948

INDEX

Some Classics from Anvil